Cat Toile

In 7 Simple Steps Like Princess Peanut Did...

The Nelson Family

(#ThePean: RetroPean)

Contents

Copyright

inattention or otherwise, by any usage or abuse of any policies, processes, or directions contained within is the solitary and utter responsibility of the recipient reader. Under no circumstances will any legal responsibility or blame be held against the publisher for any reparation, damages, or monetary loss due to the information herein, either directly or indirectly.

Respective authors own all copyrights not held by the publisher.

The information herein is offered for informational purposes solely, and is universal as so. The presentation of the information is without contract or any type of guarantee assurance.

The trademarks that are used are without any consent, and the publication of the trademark is without permission or backing by the trademark owner. All trademarks and brands within this book are for clarifying purposes only and are the owned by the owners themselves, not affiliated with this document.

INTRODUCTION

Are You Ready to Toilet Train Your Cat?

Look at that cutesy little furry face! And the teeny tiny paws! And adorable little pink nose! And… that steaming pile of sand-covered shit!

Cats are one of the greatest pets on earth and offer endless hours of cuddles and entertainment, but their biggest downfall? Stinky litter boxes. Who knew that something that precious could produce such gut-wrenching stenches from its cute little butt?

Cleaning the litter box is undoubtedly the worst aspect of being a cat owner. If you live in a city and have an indoor cat, you'll have similar feelings about the little poop-machine too. Not to mention the cost of the litter and cleaning supplies which can amount to thousands of dollars over the years. Pets are priceless, sure, but it would be nice if they didn't cost so much…

Litter boxes and the stench that comes from them is something we just put up with because we love our felines so much! But NOW there is a better way- Cat Toilet Training.

Kitty toilet training has become more and more popular in recent years as pet owners realise that it is possible to teach an old cat new tricks. The process is in fact really simple; over a number of weeks or months you encourage your cat to do their business in water rather than cat litter. It takes time, patience and a little extra love and attention. Although, it's achievable and totally worth it when you consider the money saved in the long term.

When my husband and I moved to Vancouver recently, we bought a condo in the Yaletown area. Since we had been married, (about 2 years at that time), we had always wanted a kitten. Our only reservation about getting one was the litter box that came with a cat. Since we lived in such a small space, we really didn't have an ideal place to put one and we would be constantly cleaning it. After researching about cat toilet training and how to do it, we bought a CitiKitty Toilet Trainer on Amazon.com and never looked back! The process was fairly easy and now our kitty cat Miss Peanut is dropping her bombs in the toilet and everything is cleaned with a flick of the wrist (or a flush).

Since Peanut has been trained, our household is now a litter-free one! It's less smelly, we save money, and there are no arguments about who has to clean the shitty cat sandpit each day. We're so proud of our little Princess Peanut that we want to share our experiences with you.

Toilet training can be broken down into 7 key steps, and you'll find each one right here in this book. We'll explain what each step entails, including instructions on how to use any toilet toilet training system to make the process easier (This isn't to plug a system, but we will reference Citikitty it since it worked for us) and we'll throw in some crucial tips and tricks that we learned along the way.

Ready for a litter-free home and super-smart toilet-trained cat?

Be Prepared: It's Simple, but Needs Patience.

Toilet training your cat takes time. We can't stress this enough. Cats are creatures of habit and naturally feel distrustful of new situations that put them out of their comfort zone. Moving from a litter tray on the ground to a bowl of water in the sky (at least from a cat's eye view) is a big adjustment, so the key is to move slowly so as not to freak your poor little kitty out. Here are a few words of advice before you even get started.

1. Make sure you're around as much as possible during training

Of course we all have jobs and lives, and we're not expecting you to stay home permanently for months during the training process. However, you are going to want to keep an eye on your cat's behaviour. You need to figure out how they're feeling to avoid stress. You want to check they're still going as regularly as before. You'll want to flush the toilet often to keep smells at bay. And lastly, just having you around may help your cat stay calm if they're feeling unsure about their bathroom arrangements. Try to be around as much as is sensible, and don't take any long trips away during this stage.

Our little kitten Peanut, at a very young age waited for us to come home before she went and did her business. As she got older, she began to wait until we walked in the door just so we could catch her in the act and reward her with treats. Your kitty may also do this as well. They are smarter than you think.

Be patient

Toilet training takes time. Each of the 7 stages outlined here could take anywhere between a couple of days and several weeks. Each cat is different, and we hope yours will take to the throne like a duck to water, but be prepared for this to be a long process, and don't get frustrated if your cat has accidents along the way, because we guarantee they will. This is all part of the learning curve and things will fall into place eventually.

3. **Prepare all your resources in advance**

The Essentials Are:

Flushable Cat Litter   Dust Free Light Paper Style

Cat Treats a-Plenty   #ThePean Only Eats Party Mix

A Training Kit   CitiKitty, Litter Kwitter, etc.

Catnip   Just about any type will do!

Be Ready for Training Yourself

It's not just the cat in training here; it's the owner too. You may need to change some of your habits to accommodate the kitty. That means sharing your bathroom, leaving doors open, keeping toilet lids up and flushing regularly after your cat. In each of our 7 steps we'll outline Kitty Training and Human Training so you know what you should be doing to help the process along.

(#ThePean: Getting her footing right...)

Summary of the 7 Steps

Once you're mentally and physically prepared for the toilet training rollercoaster ride, it's time to get started. To begin with, we'll briefly outline the 7 key steps below so you can become familiar with the process.

Step 1: Gradually move your cat's litter tray towards the toilet so they get into the habit of heading in that direction when it's time to go.

Step 2: Gradually raise the litter tray up from the floor until it reaches the same height as the toilet.

Step 3: Move the litter tray up onto the toilet seat; your pooping area is now the cat's pooping area.

Step 4: Replace the litter tray with the CitiKitty Training seat and fill it with flushable cat litter.

Step 5: Remove the first ring from the Training Seat so that kitty gets used to going in water.

Step 6: Gradually remove all other rings from the Training Seat to allow your cat to adjust to balancing on the toilet.

Step 7: Remove the Training Seat altogether. Celebrate with treats (& Catnip)!

Sound simple enough? It is in theory, but there are a few more tricks of the trade which we'll fill you in on along the way.

(#ThePean: Poopin' Ain't Easy!!!)

CHAPTER 1: Step 1 - Sharing the Bathroom

Objective: Gradually move the litter tray towards the toilet

Kitty Training

As mentioned previously, cats are creatures of habit. They also have an incredible sense of smell. They recognise the scent of their litter tray and know where to head when Mother Nature calls.

As you may know, suddenly moving their litter tray from one area to another can confuse them, and as a result they may have accidents in places they shouldn't, or worse still they may avoid going altogether which over time can cause health problems.

It is important to gradually move the litter tray to ensure they can see and smell it from where their usual spot is. Move it a little further each day until you reach the bathroom, and don't stop there.

You need to get the litter tray as close to the toilet as possible. Most cats dislike water and a huge bowl full of water seems particularly scary to them (Although #ThePean is a strange one). She used to try and jump in our condo's pond when we walked her outside and she insisted on her being in the bathroom while someone was taking a shower to hear the water dropping. Weird- we just think she's a country girl.

Anyway- the bathroom may smell strongly of cleaning products such as bleach, as well as soaps and shampoos. Your cat needs to become familiar with all of these smells in order to feel comfortable doing their stuff in the toilet. Encouraging them to use their litter tray near to the toilet will make a huge difference to their progress.

At the time when you start moving your kitty's litter box- mix in some flushable litter with the regular litter. Gradually put more and more flushable litter compared to regular litter in their litter box until it is all full of the flushable type. As said before, cats don't always love change- so introducing flushable litter slowly will be helpful in the process of toilet training. We used the "World's Best Cat Litter" from Walmart which is completely flushable. Do not make the mistake of flushing regular litter, as you will clog your toilet up!

Human Training

Leave the bathroom door open at all times. Although some particularly sneaky cats are skilled in turning door handles, most aren't and they need to be able to wander in and out of the bathroom as they please. Don't just leave it ajar either; open it the whole way so that it doesn't seem like a scary, unfamiliar place.

Be prepared to share the bathroom with your feline friend. It can be confusing for them to have the litter tray locked away for long periods, and this could lead to unwanted accidents. If you're partial to long baths or showers you may have to leave the door open so your cat knows it can reach its litter tray when it needs it.

Alternatively, cut the time you spend locked in the bathroom to a minimum whilst they're still learning how to share the bathroom with you. Cats are pretty private creatures when it comes to doing their business though, so you shouldn't have to deal with them stinking up the place whilst you enjoy a hot soak in the tub.

(#ThePean relaxing after tough poo...)

CHAPTER 2: Step 2 - Take it Higher

Objective: Raise the litter box until it is at the same height as the toilet.

Kitty Training

Would you like to hover your butt over a ledge whilst you try to do your business? No, didn't think so. Your cat doesn't want to either. But you can prepare them for it and the first step is to raise the litter box up, bit by bit, until your cat is familiar with using it at a similar height to the toilet.

The crucial thing here is that you do it very gradually. Cats love to climb and like they being up high (we all know they love being the superior beings of the household), but it's strange for them to suddenly go from using their litter box on the ground to using it at heights. Increase it by no more than around 5cm each time.

Try to observe their behaviour. They may seem a little unsure at first, but after a few days it should be like normal. Each time you raise the litter box up, check to see that they're still using it regularly and not leaving little gifts elsewhere around the house. This is a clear sign that they're distressed and don't feel comfortable using the box. If this is the case, lower the tray again until they get the hang of it. We said you'd need patience, right? Catnip may help keep the cat attracted to the litter box or the bathroom that the litter box is in. Peanut is a total druggie when it comes to Catnip- she goes crazy for it! So when we wanted to get her back on track we sprinkled some around the toilet seat and in her litter.

Another key point to mention is that your ever-growing litter tray platform needs to be safe and secure. It can't wobble. The tray shouldn't slip and slide beneath your cat when they jump up. Not only will this make them daunted about using it, but it will also leave a lovely mess if it does topple over.

You could stack up heavy books, use wooden crates or boxes, or even use a small table providing that it's wide enough. Ensure there enough surface area on the platform around the litter tray that your cat can move around it with ease. You may also want to cover it with a sheet or towel in order to prevent the surface from being slippery.

Human Training

Make sure the litter box remains as close to the toilet during this stage, and try to leave the toilet lid up and the seat down. Not only is it helpful for you to get into this habit now, but it will also encourage the cat to climb onto the toilet since it's at the same level as the litter box. The more familiar they get with that big, porcelain water bowl and the less scary it will seem.

(#ThePean Can Poop Just Like You)

CHAPTER 3: Step 3 - Toilet Time

Objective: Move the litter tray onto the toilet seat

Kitty Training

Now your cat can use their litter tray at a greater height, it shouldn't be too tricky to simply move the tray onto the toilet itself. Again though, there is the risk of the tray slipping, so you may need to use some boxes or books stacked either side of the toilet so that the tray doesn't wobble. An old sheet or towel can prevent it slipping, too.

You may find this step isn't too much of an adjustment for your cat and that they take to it really quickly. This, obviously, is great, but don't be tempted to move onto the next step too quickly. Moving from a regular litter box to the Training Seat litter box in the next section is quite a step for your feline. Give it a good few days, looking out for any signs of distress or accidents around the house. When you're really, really sure your cat is ready, move on.

We used 1 week of no accidents as a marker that Peanut was ready to move on to the next step.

Human Training

This is perhaps the most inconvenient step for you; having to move the litter tray, along with any sheets or platforms blocking your way, each time you need to use the toilet. It's worth it though, and hopefully this step shouldn't go on for too long, either.

The key thing here is do not, for the love of cats, forget to put the tray back on the toilet seat when you're done. You've come a long way in these 3 steps, and if you end up accidentally leaving the litter box on the floor you will risk confusing the poor cat who has just got used to hopping up onto the loo to go. This could set you back days or weeks, and we don't want that.

(#ThePean Will Not Pee in This Hot Laundry)

CHAPTER 4: Step 4 - It's CitiKitty Time (or your preference of another system)

Objective: Cat uses Training Seat instead of normal litter box.

Kitty Training

The time has come for CitiKitty to take over from that much hated litter box. Here's how it works.

The system is comprised of a Training Seat which has 6 removable rings. The seat sits in the bowl of the toilet and is filled with cat litter. To begin with, the Training Seat remains whole; don't remove any rings. This allows your cat to get used to a smaller, toilet-sized litter tray. During this stage the cat doesn't have to worry about balancing too much. It's likely that they will become used to hovering on the toilet seat, but since the CitiKitty seat is sturdy enough they can crouch as normal, with all four paws securely in the litter tray. Once again, check for any signs of distress in your cat or a change in their toileting habits and don't move on until you think the cat seems content using this new type of litter tray. Use some catnip for a little extra help at this stage.

Human Training

This step is pretty easy. You only need to remember to remove the CitiKitty Seat before you use the toilet…

In all seriousness, it's pretty easy to remove it and you can get into the habit of flushing the contents of the tray away each time you go to the bathroom – remember you should be flushing regularly when your cat is fully toilet trained as they don't like the smell of their own business.

We found it helpful to have a dustpan and brush in the bathroom so that any litter that was kicked off of the toilet can be easily cleaned right away. If not, we ran the risk of Peanut using litter on the ground as her litter box!

One more thing; when the CitiKitty is in place, the toilet seat lid cannot be closed. Make sure you leave the lid up at all times for your cat, and let guests know what's going on too so they don't make the same mistake. It may even be useful to tape the lid up if possible so you don't risk accidentally locking the tray away from your cat.

Here are some Cat Toilet Training Systems for Your Reference:

CitiKitty: This is the system we used to train Peanut. This system is disposable after use. She was fully trained in about 6 weeks. We started training her when she was about four months old. You place the system in the toilet and then as your kitten progresses (we used 1 week without accidents as our marker), you remove a ring in the system. The end result is the last ring then being removed and moving solely to the toilet seat with a sprinkle of litter on it.

with **DVD** VIDEO instructions

Litter Kwitter: This system uses reusable coloured rings. As your cat progresses through the toilet training process, you remove a ring. The benefit of this system is if your cat makes mistakes and has to "re-do" a level, you can re insert a ring easily. If you need to train future feline friends- You can do that as well!

(#ThePean Making Progress with 2 of her CitiKitty Rings Out)

CHAPTER 5: Step 5 - The Teeny Tiny Toilet Bowl

Objective: Remove the first ring from the CitiKitty Training Seat

Kitty Training

When you remove the first, smallest ring from the CitiKitty Seat it may seem as though it doesn't make too much difference. The hole is very small and still doesn't look much like a real toilet, but the subtle change will be noticed by your cat. They will be aware of avoiding the hole when manoeuvring on the seat, and will become used to their waste dropping into water.

By removing just the smallest ring first, you're allowing them to get to grips with these changes without having to worry about balancing too much just yet. The amount of time it will take them to adjust will depend on your cat; it could be a few days or it could take much longer. Be on hand with treats to reinforce their behaviour when they successfully use the toilet. Again add a little catnip to the litter at this stage.

Human Training

When removing the rings from the CitiKitty, it is often a good idea to limit your cat's access to other rooms. This means that if they feel unsure about using the toilet, they have limited options of other places to go to do their business. Keep that bathroom door wide open and even if they are a little nervous about using the toilet they'll realise that room is meant for them, and the litter tray over the toilet is the only logical place to go.

(#ThePean Owning the Bathroom...)

CHAPTER 6: Step 6 – Remove ALL the Rings!

Objective: Gradually remove all the rings from the CitiKitty Seat

Kitty Training

During Stage 6 your cat will have to master the art of toilet seat balancing. Cats are gymnasts but it still may be tricky for them to perch on the edge of seat, but it's the feeling of doing their business into water that they need to become mostly familiar with.

Once again, slow and steady wins the race here. There's no need to rush removing the rings and often it's best to do it over a number of weeks or couple of months rather than days so that you don't overwhelm the cat. And always remember, a little catnip can always help. Once again, we used 1 week without any accidents with Peanut as a marker to move to the next step (the removal of the next ring). Especially for the first 3 steps, Peanut only took about 1 week to get her footing right. By the last few steps, we took about 10 days to 2 weeks at each ring. Trust us, the wait is worth it! Once your kitty gets it- you will come home to pee and poo in the potty where they belong!

With each ring removed, the less litter you will be using. The bonus is that you're already saving money on expensive cat litter, but the downside for your cat is that the familiar litter smell will become less and less, particularly if most of their waste ends up in the toilet bowl rather than in the litter. This is why this step can be particularly tricky and will no doubt take the longest. Patience is key.

We saved so much money on litter when training Peanut! Throughout the entire training process we only used 1 bag of "Worlds Best Flushable Cat Litter" and still had some left over for reinforcement when the CitiKitty was removed!

Human Training

Observing your cat's behaviour during this stage is crucial. If they seem lost looking for their litter tray or start to leave little presents elsewhere around your home, it may be wise to take a couple of steps back. Add in more rings so that they become more comfortable using the toilet again, and wait a little longer before you progress any further.

Sometimes it can get tricky when you are babysitting another kitty. We used to take care of another kitten named Milo. He wasn't potty trained, and Peanut would get off track when he came over as he also came with a litter box. We would sometimes find accidents beside the toilet after Milo left, but with reinforcements and treats, Peanut got it again!

(SPECIAL GUEST STAR - #MilotheKitten hanging around. He is too young to be potty trained, but his mother wants to use CitiKitty and get him trained as soon as he is big enough)

CHAPTER 7: Step 7 - Bye-Bye Training Seat, Hello Toilet Trained Kitty!

Objective: Remove the Training Seat completely

Kitty Training

You're at the final hurdle. Your cat has been using the last ring of the training seat successfully and you think you're ready to take the last leap to complete freedom from cat litter. This is an awesome achievement but don't celebrate just yet.

You need to observe your cat closely at this point. With no sign of their litter in the toilet bowl, they may feel utterly confused about where to go. Remember to keep that bathroom door wide open and that toilet lid lifted at all times so they know that's their spot.

Use lots of positive reinforcement each time you've noticed that they used the toilet successfully. Don't pressure them or crowd them as cats like privacy, but observe from a distance to ensure that this last step hasn't been too soon.

If you find that your cat has stopped using the toilet at any point, don't fret. Replace the CitKitty and litter and simply work your way forwards again. Cats are strange, mysterious creatures and it's not unusual for them to suddenly change their minds and decide they're not okay with pooping on a toilet. Be patient until the time is right for them – it will happen eventually.

Human Training

Bask in the glory of being a fully qualified and successful cat toilet trainer. Just remember to flush that toilet regularly! As mentioned previously, cats don't like the strong scent of their own waste and if left too long they may avoid using the toilet. It may be useful to install an automatic flusher for when you're out for long periods. The benefit is that the smell will be reduced compared to when in the litter tray, which is great for you and your cat.

When Peanut was fully trained, we would hear her in the middle of the night tinkling in the toilet. It was so funny to wake up to- we would laugh hysterically at first, and now we sleep straight through it.

(#ThePean, All On Her Own!!!)

BONUS TIPS & TRICKS

The chapters above outline the key steps involved in toilet training, but here are a few extra snippets of advice that you'll probably find handy along the journey.

Switch plastic or resin toilet seats for wooden or padded alternatives

Cats can balance on the teeniest, tiniest of areas, but sometimes shiny surfaces are their worst enemy and make them lose their cool as their feet slip from underneath them. Plastic toilet seats can be really slippery, and you don't want to risk your cat falling into the toilet bowl as a result. Trust us, it can happen. Not only could it be scary for them, but this risk may also make them too nervous to successfully toilet train.

Wooden or padded toilet seats offer a little more grip, making for a safer pooping platform than plastic seats. Once your cat has investigated the toilet seat and found it's not too slippery, they'll feel more confident balancing up there. Think about your toilet seat before you start training, or at least before you install the training seat so that your cat can feel confident from the first time the step on there.

Moving home soon? Start toilet training in your new place

Your cat may associate new toilet habits with a changed environment and take more quickly to the training than when doing it in a familiar home. Obviously not everyone can move house just to toilet train their kitty, but if you're considering training because of an upcoming move - maybe you're moving to the city where your cat won't be able to go outdoors to roam, or you simply don't want specks of cat litter scattered all over your brand new floors (that stuff gets everywhere!) - then make the most of it and get that cat trained.

Once your cat is toilet trained you should be aware that it will be hard on them should you move home. You may have to temporarily move back to a litter tray or to the CitiKitty temporarily whilst they get used to their new environment and a new toilet. Some cats will adapt quickly, others will take a little longer; just be patient whilst they settle in to their new home.

Hide optimum peeing and pooping spots during toilet training

Cats love soil in potted plants and this is a far more attractive place to go than they tall, scary toilet. The bath mats also look like a great place to go. In fact any rug in any other room is more tempting than the weird new litter tray you're encouraging him to use.

It's natural that your cat will look for a more comfortable place to go if feeling unsure about the toilet, so during training try to keep access to these places to a minimum. Cover soil in indoor plants with aluminium foil and remove rugs or mats throughout the house. Keep doors to most other rooms closed to prevent your cat finding secret spots to use, too. By the time they finish their training they should feel comfortable with using the toilet and the risk of accidents should be reduced.

Toilet train kittens when they reach 3 months

It may be tempting to try to train your little kitten as soon as possible into using the toilet, but in reality it's not very practical. Kittens first need to understand that there is a particular spot where they are allowed to do their business. Training them to use a litter tray is far easier than starting them off with toilet training and will instil this basic principle into them.

Once your kitten is successfully litter trained you can move them onto toilet training and, due to their young age, they're likely to learn relatively quickly.

Don't give up on your old cat – they can learn too!

Cats of any age can be taught how to toilet train, so don't worry that yours is too old to pick up new habits. If you've lived in the same home and had their litter tray in the same place for many years, each of our 7 steps may take a little longer, but they're still more than capable of being successfully toilet trained.

If your cat has health conditions related to their age, however, such as arthritis, kidney problems or urinary problems, it's not recommended to toilet train them. Manoeuvring up to the toilet may be impossible for them, and interrupting their normal toileting routine could be more damaging to their health. If in any doubt about whether to toilet train your cat for these reasons, consult your vet.

CONCLUSION

We know this will help toilet train your cat with ease. Start applying what you've learned right away and the sooner you will have a litter free home.

Finally, if you enjoyed this book, then we'd like to ask you for a favor, would you be kind enough to leave a review for this book on Amazon? As you can see above, The Pean will really appreciate it!

Thank you and good luck!

The Nelson Family

Resources For Cat Toilet Training:

1. Litter Kwitter Toilet Trainer

2. Automatic Toilet Flusher

3. CitiKitty Toilet Trainer

4. Flushable Cat Litter

5. Party Mix (#ThePean Preferred)

(#ThePean: Giant Cat Takes Over VanCity)

More Books By The Nelson Family:

Make Your Cat The Best Cat Ever...(3 Titles in 1)

1. Cat Toilet Training: In 7 Simple Steps

2. Cat Names: Female, Male & Other Cute Cat Names

3. Cat Care: Exactly How to Make Your Cat Feel Like a Million Buck$

Cat Care: Make Your Cat Feel Like a Million Buck$

What You Will Learn:

- 3 Main Care Areas: Ear Care, Nail Care, & Grooming/Skin Care...

- After Reading This Book, You Will Know Signs of Illness in Your Cat...

- You Will Learn How to Properly Check for Ear Mites & Trim Your Cat's Nails in a SAFE Way!

- Discussion on the Controversial Topic of Declawing & other methods that will help keep your awesome furniture looking brand new...

- After learning some tips to trim your cat's nails... your friends might start calling you "the cat whisperer"...

Cat Names: Female, Male & Other Names For Your Favourite Feline

Here Are the Types of Names We Will Explore:

- The Classic Cat – Classic cat names which remain timeless for years...

- The Distinguished Feline – Posh, regal titles to suit purebred cats...

- The Mangy Cat – Cat names for the weird, scruffy, one-of-a-kind cats.

- The Impersonator – Human names for cats who think they're one of us.

- The Character Cat – Names for cats taken from character in movies or TV shows to allow endless hours of entertainment.

- The Celebri-Kitty – Cat names for diva cats worthy of the red carpet.

33923604R00033

Made in the USA
Lexington, KY
16 March 2019